DO YOU KNOW?

Level 4

SPACE

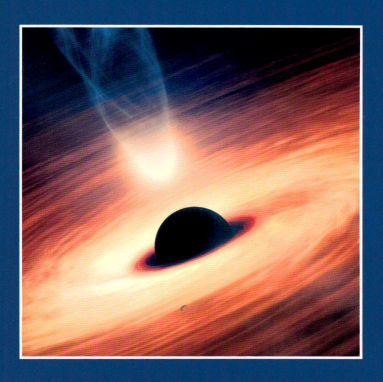

Written by Hannah Fish
Series Editor: Nick Coates
Designed by Dynamo Limited

LADYBIRD BOOKS

UK | USA | Canada | Ireland | Australia
India | New Zealand | South Africa

Ladybird Books Ltd is part of the Penguin Random House group of companies
whose addresses can be found at global.penguinrandomhouse.com.
www.penguin.co.uk   www.puffin.co.uk   www.ladybird.co.uk

Penguin
Random House
UK

First published 2023
001

Text copyright © Ladybird Books Ltd, 2023

Printed in China

The authorized representative in the EEA is Penguin Random House Ireland,
Morrison Chambers, 32 Nassau Street, Dublin D02 YH68

A CIP catalogue record for this book is available from the British Library

ISBN: 978-0-241-62258-2

All correspondence to:
Ladybird Books
Penguin Random House Children's
One Embassy Gardens, 8 Viaduct Gardens, London SW11 7BW

Contents

New words

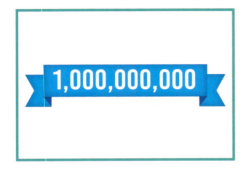

billion

connect

galaxy

gravity

huge

life

object
(noun)

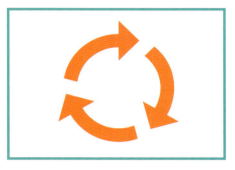

rotate / rotation
(verb) / (noun)

scientist

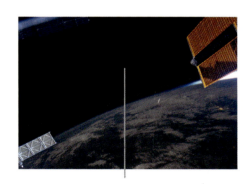

space

star

surface

Where does our Solar System end?

Mercury, Venus, Earth and Mars are the first four planets in our Solar System. Then there is the asteroid belt. The planets Jupiter, Saturn, Uranus and Neptune are next.

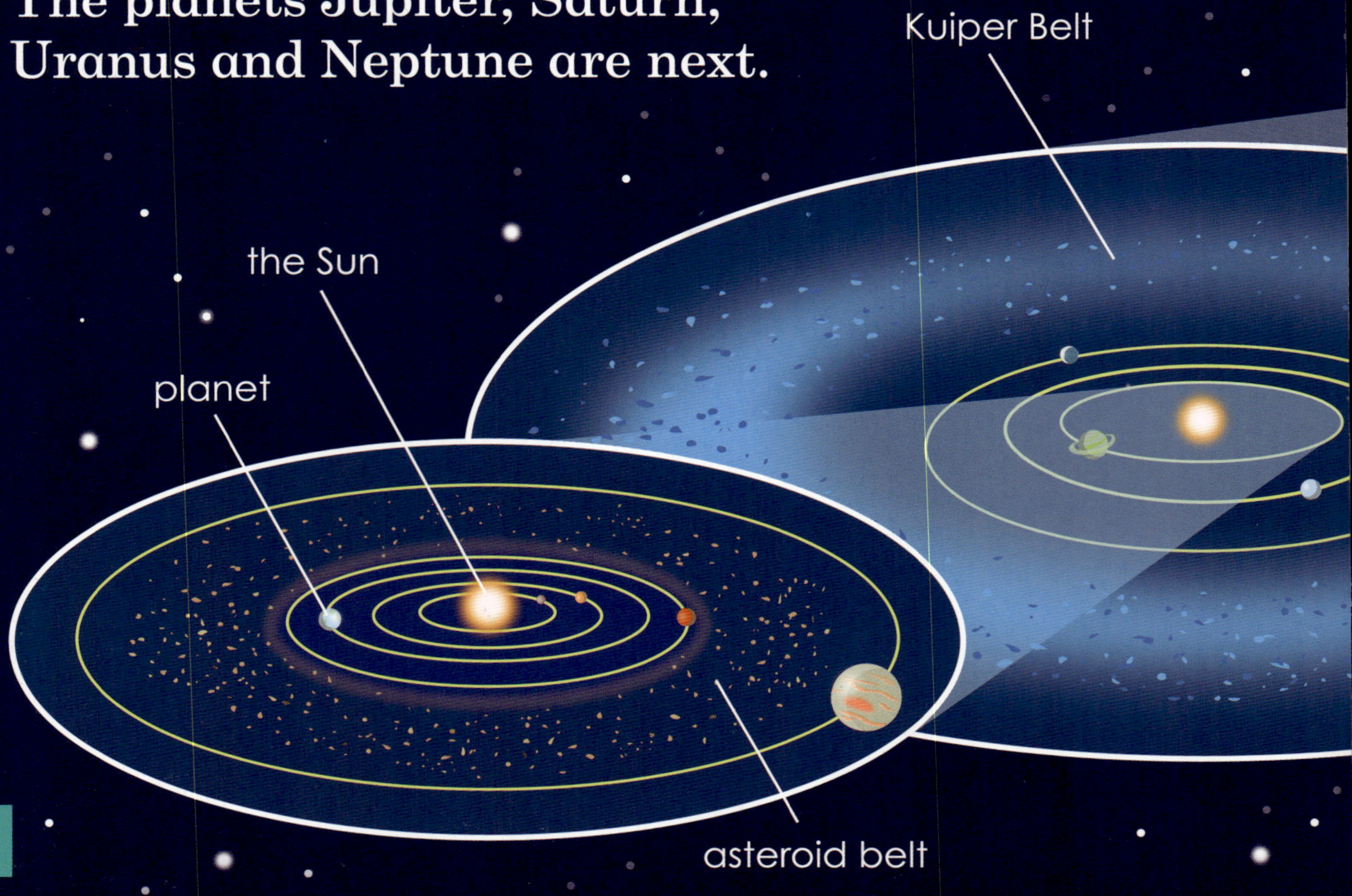

Kuiper Belt

the Sun

planet

asteroid belt

After Neptune is the Kuiper Belt. There are **billions** of asteroids, comets and small planets in the Kuiper Belt. Outside all of this is the Oort Cloud – a **huge** cloud of billions of **objects** at the end of our Solar System!

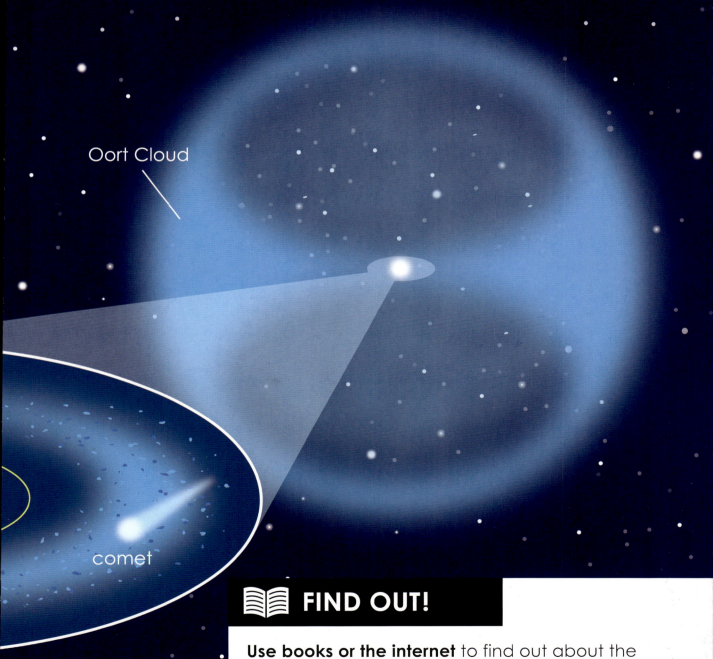

Oort Cloud

comet

📖 FIND OUT!

Use books or the internet to find out about the Oort Cloud. Scientists have never seen objects in the Oort Cloud, but they think it is real. Why?

Are there planets like Earth?

Earth is home to millions of animals and plants, but are there other planets like Earth? Earth is in the habitable zone of our Solar System. This is the part of a solar system where **life** can grow. It is not too hot or too cold, so planets in this zone can have water on their **surface**.

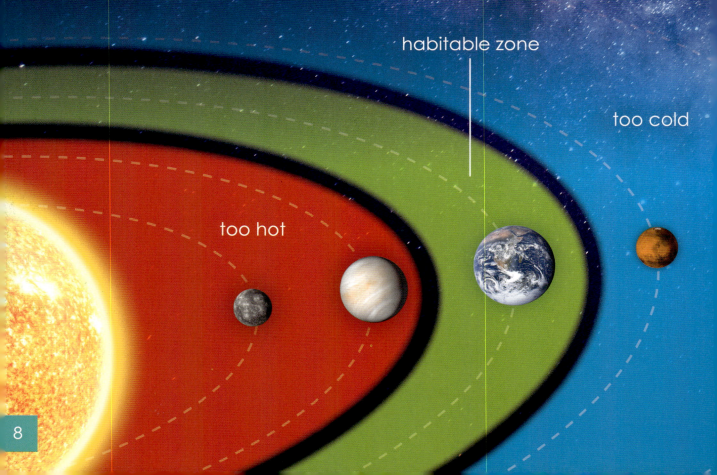

habitable zone

too cold

too hot

In 2015, a planet called Kepler-452b was found in the habitable zone of its solar system.

Kepler-452b is called 'Earth's older, bigger cousin'.

Earth

Kepler-452b

We don't know if there is life on Kepler-452b.

life

 **THINK!**

Would you like to live on another planet? Give reasons for your answer.

How do we know that Earth is moving?

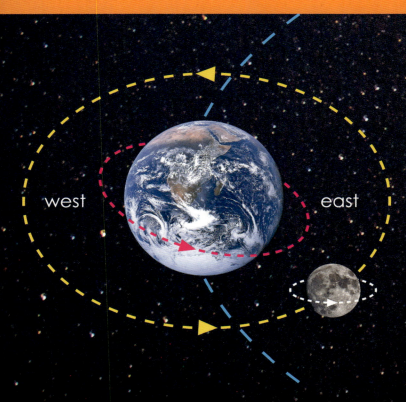

west

east

Every day, the Sun and Moon come up in the east and move across the sky to the west. Watching this is how people first understood that Earth **rotates**, and that a full **rotation** takes 24 hours. Earth also travels around the Sun. It takes one year.

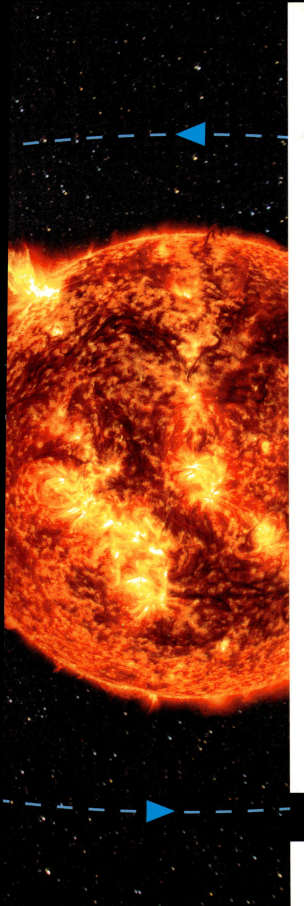

Cheetahs run at 121 kilometres an hour. Earth rotates at 1,675 kilometres an hour!

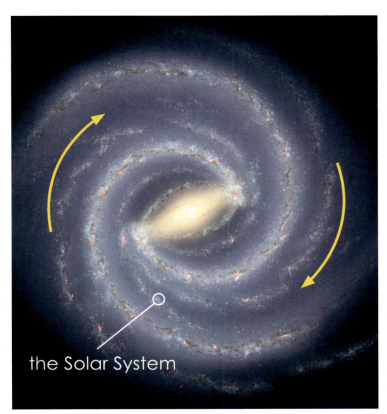

the Solar System

Our Solar System travels around the centre of our **galaxy**, the Milky Way.

 **PROJECT**

Work with a friend. Make a poster about the different ways Earth moves.

How fast can we go?

The fastest plane can travel at about 7,200 kilometres an hour, but what about spacecraft – how fast can they go?

astronaut

The astronauts in the Apollo 10 spacecraft travelled at 39,897 kilometres an hour as they came back to Earth from the Moon.

That is fast, but a spacecraft without astronauts can go faster.

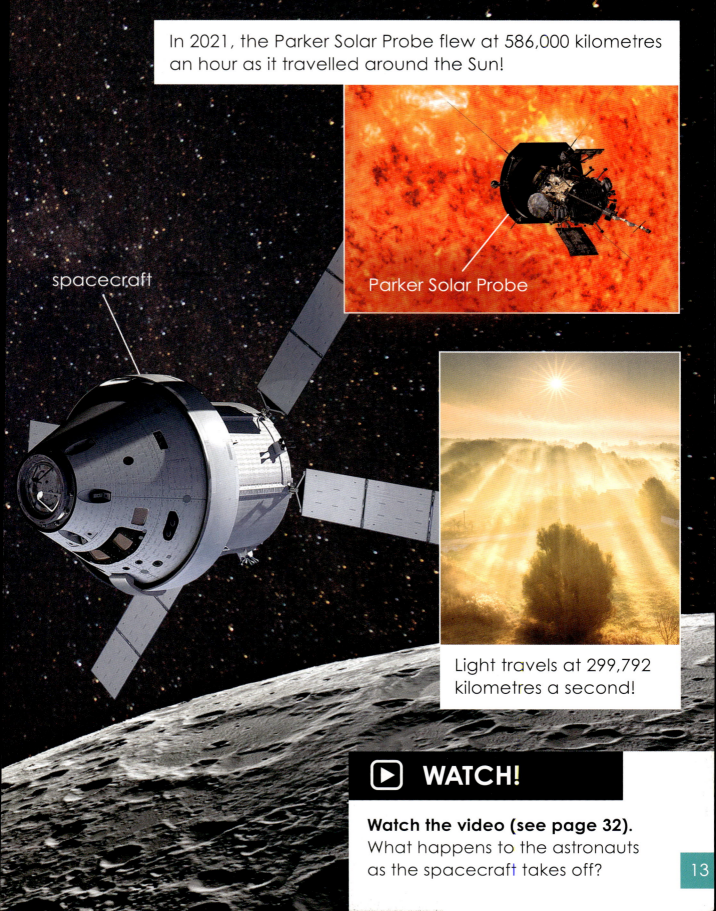

In 2021, the Parker Solar Probe flew at 586,000 kilometres an hour as it travelled around the Sun!

Parker Solar Probe

spacecraft

Light travels at 299,792 kilometres a second!

▶ **WATCH!**

Watch the video (see page 32).
What happens to the astronauts as the spacecraft takes off?

13

How far can we go?

Wormholes are an exciting idea! A wormhole takes you from one place in **space** to another place in space, or from one point in time to another point in time.

Hermann Weyl had the idea of a wormhole in 1928.

Wormholes **connect** places and times that are far from each other. If there are wormholes, we can use them to travel around space faster than light. But we do not know if there are wormholes!

We see wormholes in films.

We make spacecrafts that go far. This is Voyager 1. It is at the end of the Solar System. It can travel far and tell us more about space.

 **FIND OUT!**

Use books or the internet to find out more about Hermann Weyl.

What is a black hole?

A black hole is a part of space where **gravity** is very strong. The gravity stops the light getting out. This means that we cannot see black holes or see inside them. We use telescopes in space and on Earth to help us find black holes.

Space telescopes watch how **stars** and other space objects move near black holes.

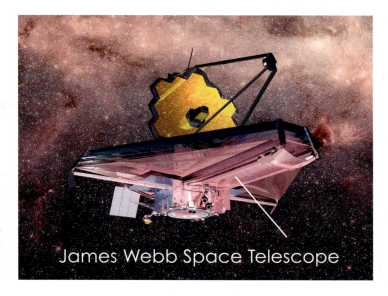

James Webb Space Telescope

Many black holes are made when a huge star dies in a supernova explosion.

supernova explosion

Scientists have found a black hole that is 13.1 billion years old!

 WATCH!

Watch the video (see page 32).
How do the colours change as the black hole is created?

17

A black hole's gravity is very strong, so it pulls stars and other space objects into it. These objects break into pieces as they travel into the black hole, and they make the black hole grow bigger.

Black holes can grow very big. The biggest are called supermassive black holes. Millions, or even billions, of suns can go into supermassive black holes.

centre

Supermassive black holes are found at the centre of big galaxies.

There is a supermassive black hole at the centre of the Milky Way.

📋 PROJECT

Work with a friend. Make a fact file about the supermassive black hole at the centre of the Milky Way.

Is there life on Mars?

Today, Mars is too cold and dry for things to live, but we know that in the past it was wetter and a little warmer. There were places on the surface of Mars where life could grow.

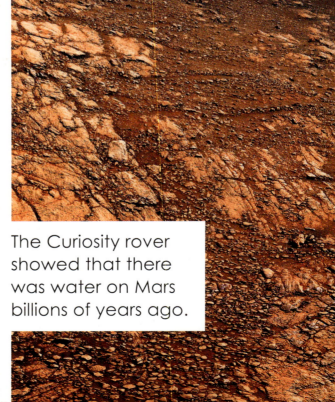

The Curiosity rover showed that there was water on Mars billions of years ago.

Was there life in the water on Mars in the past? The Perseverance rover is studying Jezero crater to find out.

crater

Jezero crater had lots of water in the past.

▶ **WATCH!**

Watch the video (see page 32).
What did we find on Mars?

How big are the biggest stars?

the Sun

UY Scuti

All stars are big, but the really huge stars are the hypergiant stars. 1.3 million Earths can go inside the Sun, but it is only a small star.

Giant, supergiant and hypergiant stars are all much bigger than the Sun. The biggest star we know about is a hypergiant called UY Scuti. Five billion suns can go inside it!

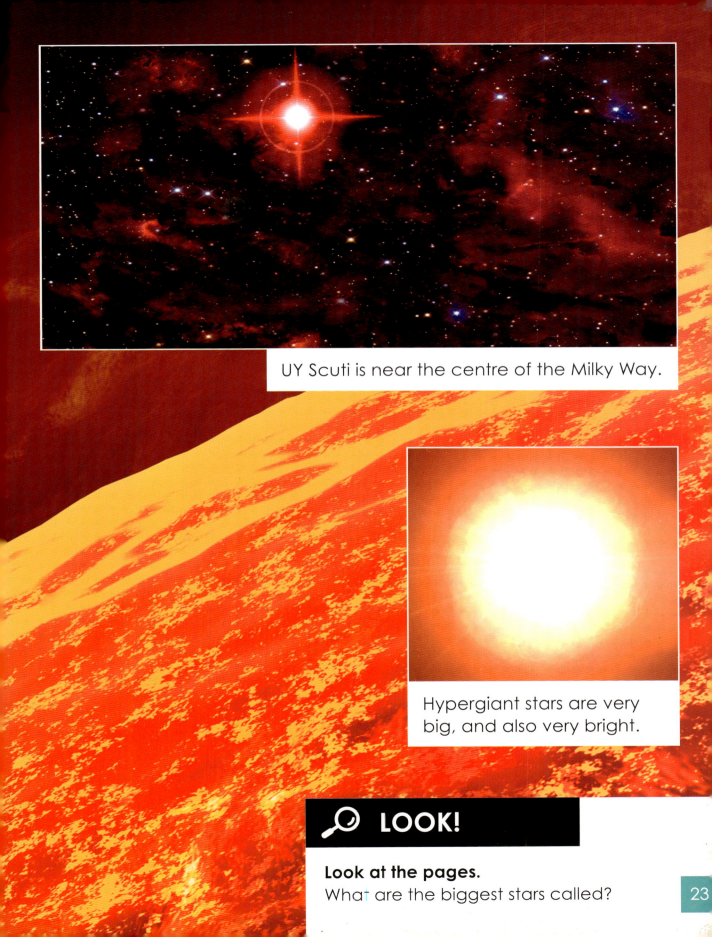

UY Scuti is near the centre of the Milky Way.

Hypergiant stars are very big, and also very bright.

🔍 LOOK!

Look at the pages.
What are the biggest stars called?

23

How heavy can a star be?

The Sun is 330,000 times heavier than Earth, but many stars are much heavier than the Sun.

A hypergiant star called Eta Carinae A is 150 times heavier than the Sun! Scientists think that in the next 100,000 years, Eta Carinae A will die in a supernova explosion.

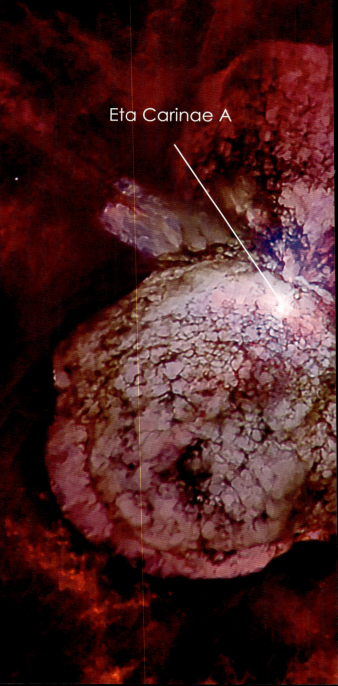

Eta Carinae A

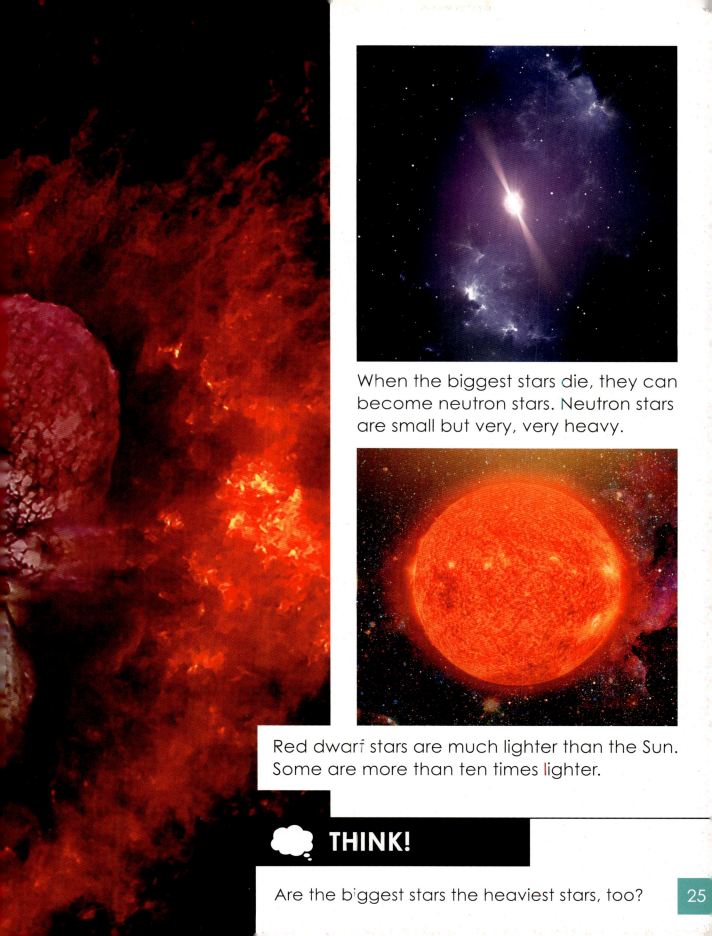

When the biggest stars die, they can become neutron stars. Neutron stars are small but very, very heavy.

Red dwarf stars are much lighter than the Sun. Some are more than ten times lighter.

💭 **THINK!**

Are the biggest stars the heaviest stars, too?

What is a rogue planet?

Most planets travel around
a star in a solar system,
but some planets don't.
They are called rogue planets.
Some rogue planets travel
around a galaxy, but
others travel between
galaxies in space.

Rogue planets are cold and dark because they are not near a star.

rogue star

There are also rogue stars. Rogue stars are not in galaxies.

💭 **THINK!**

Is Earth a rogue planet? How do you know?

Can we see dark matter?

There are galaxies, stars, planets, black holes, comets and asteroids in space. There is dark matter between them.

We can't see dark matter, but we know it is there. We can see it pulling on objects like stars and galaxies, so we know it has gravity. But it is not a black hole. We don't know what it is, but we want to find out!

The Large Hadron Collider can help us to understand dark matter.

Space telescopes can help us to understand dark matter, too.

 **FIND OUT!**

Use books or the internet to find out how scientists study dark matter.

Quiz

Choose the correct answers.

1 There are billions of . . . in the Oort Cloud.
  a planets
  b objects
  c solar systems

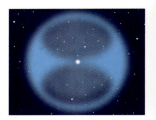

2 Earth rotates at . . . kilometres an hour.
  a 1,675
  b 121
  c 24

3 Hermann Weyl had the idea of
a wormhole in . . .
  a 1981.
  b 2007.
  c 1928.

4 A black hole's gravity is . . .
  a cold.
  b strong.
  c weak.

5 Hypergiant stars are . . .

   a small stars.

   b dark stars.

   c huge stars.

6 Red dwarf stars are . . . than the Sun.

   a lighter

   b heavier

   c hotter

7 . . . planets do not travel around a star.

   a Rogue

   b Dwarf

   c Big

8 We . . . dark matter.

   a will see

   b can see

   c can't see

Visit www.ladybirdeducation.co.uk for FREE DO YOU KNOW? teaching resources.

- video clips with simplified voiceover and subtitles
- video and comprehension activities
- class projects and lesson plans
- audio recording of every book
- digital version of every book
- full answer keys

To access video clips, audio tracks and digital books:

1 Go to **www.ladybirdeducation.co.uk**
2 Click 'Unlock book'
3 Enter the code below

ka72S3W4QP

Stay safe online! Some of the DO YOU KNOW? activities ask children to do extra research online. Remember:

- ensure an adult is supervising;
- use established search engines such as Google or Kiddle;
- children should never share personal details, such as name, home or school address, telephone number or photos.